Tomorrow is Coming

Jennifer Rak

BookLeaf Publishing

Presentation by *BookLeaf Publishing*

Web: www.bookleafpub.com

E-mail: info@bookleafpub.com

ISBN: 978-93-95784-90-0

First edition 2022

Heavy Eyes and Tired Hearts

The book sits in my lap.

This book, isn't just a book.
It's the book.

My favorite one.

The one where the storyline swallows me whole,
stealing me from a reality that feels counterfeit.
Leaving me eternally thankful for the small
reprieve.

I feel grounded and free while devouring the
words that take me away.

But tonite, I stay here.
Very present.
Anchored to this reality.

It's not that I can't read it.
It's just that I can't read it.

Aimlessly, I pet the cover and trace the raised
letters of the title.

Open the cover and stare at the well loved
sentences for hours that feel like minutes.

The words are a puzzle I can't put together
today.

I cry.

Less than last time,
but still a lot.

I slide the book from the protection of my ample
thighs and let it hit the floor.

I sigh, I'm sorry, as I hear the thud.

My head sinks into the pillow, again.

Again because I've lost count and really don't
want to know how many times I've crawled back
into my bed, into my hole to get away from my
head.

I pull the covers up to my chin.
No sighs.
No dreams.
Just darkness.

Tonite, I need the darkness.

Or maybe the darkness needs me to hold it tight
because people always choose the light.

I don't know but my eyes are heavy and my
heart is tired.

Maybe tomorrow I whisper to my tales tossed on
the floor.

Maybe tomorrow.

Bridge Prayers

My mother always prayed when we crossed a bridge over water.

"It's good luck", she'd barely breathe while her white knuckles grasped the steering wheel.

"You just don't know. I'd rather take all the help we can get" and she would start her prayers again, chanting quietly, beseeching sweetly for safety to get home.

The prayers were silly I thought.

Bridges were enchanting.

Magic that connected lands over waters.

A steely huge bond to bring people together.

Then, one night, you looked a little too wistfully at the highest point of the bridge and let your eyes slowly trail down to the glistening water.

You wouldn't meet my eyes for days afterwards.

And I realized the prayers to get us home safely
was never silly after all.

Rufus and Zelda

My legs feel heavier than yesterday and yesterday they felt like the trunks of giant sequoias.

I drag myself up.

My feet force me to the living room.

My dogs, my tiny chihuahuas, joyfully trot to see me.

They deserve better than my slow pathetic pets I think while I stroke them behind the ears.

I bring them outside and let the sun burn my eyes as they smell the grass and mark every blade with their scent.

It's too bright today.

We go back in and I give them their treats for doing their business and wonder if I deserve a treat too.

I open the fridge and the cupboards but nothing looks good.

We retreat to the living room as a funny little trio. One barely functioning human sloth flanked by two small bursts of happy energy.

Their tiny paws dance on my belly and chest as they lick me as I lie horizontal on the couch.

Hey, at least I'm out of bed.

They calm and snuggle me like I'm the best person to love.

Like I'm worthy of love.

I snuggle them harder.

I accepted my treat for the day.

The Coldest Fire

My therapist said many things that helped me
reframe my thinking.

She said these many things many times and for
the most part they lodged in my thick skull.

One day she told me that you could have all the
skills,
the best intentions,
and all the resources but if you had caregivers
fatigue
and someone was on fire in front of you,
you would watch them burn.

I felt like I was freezing my loved ones out by
making them watch me burn.

They had fire extinguishers and blankets at the
ready
desperately trying to smother the sadness that
was spreading.

Every time they got close
I somehow dodged them
and found fuel to make my fire stronger.

I was a caretaker from a young age.

Not by choice I was not resentful but it became a part of my identity.

Now I was the one who needed help.

If I couldn't help someone how would I prove my worth?

If I couldn't show I was valuable why would they want me around?

If I couldn't improve something with my presence why be there at all?

What happens when you're watching yourself burn but also fueling the fire?

And, just why did I feel my coldest why the fire raged on?

When Food Talks

I made you breakfast.
    Please get out of bed.

I made you lunch.
    Please eat something.

I made you dinner.
    Please talk to me.

Sit by me.
    Stay here with me.

Stephanie

My coworkers brought me flowers.

Well, one person came but they were from everyone.

I was thankful that it was only one person.

She was the ambassador chosen to report back on if I was me again yet.

I wasn't.

We stood in my yard. Her eyes searched my face but not rudely, just looking for familiar territory.

I was waiting for it to be awkward.

It wasn't.

I couldn't tell you today what color those flowers were or how sweet they smelled but I could tell you they were my favorite. I desperately and protectively clung to them like they were my own personal bouquet of hope in a vase. A collection of hugs from people meaning well and rooting for me on this weird battle.

I didn't ask about work just to be polite.

She didn't force me to lie and say I was fine.

We stood saying nothing and everything in our silence.

It was the best conversation I never had.

Baby Steps

Sometimes,
I get jealous of kids.

Like,
the little ones.

I'm not proud of it,
but here we are.

The kids who get nap time,
and snacks,
and get to cuddle with their parents,
and watch cartoons.

They are encouraged to love,
to walk,
to talk,
to play.

Shoot.

Adults need that encouragement more.

Because,
as an adult,

I've lost that razzle dazzle,
and half the toys I love
are now broken,
like my heart.

Some days,
its hard to want to talk,
to engage,
to keep walking.

It's easier to hide away,
and refuse to play.

I get it.

They need it.

And they can't fend for themselves.

But,
man,
I'm going to grab a juice box
and nap
and dream about
having no responsibilities
and being celebrated for just
being.

Mechanics of Holding on

Breathing,
is much more than just in and out.

The mechanics,
are a little more precise,
a beautiful miracle
meshed with science,
it's your diaphragm contracting,
tightening,
and moving downward.

The space in your chest cavity,
will increase,
grow,
so your lungs can expand.

The muscles in between your ribs,
will also open up that chest cavity.
The muscles shrink down,
to pull your rib cage
both upward and outwards
when you inhale.

When we need to exhale,
breathe out,

your diaphragm relaxes and moves up into the
chest cavity.

Those muscles between the ribs will switch it up
now
and relax to shrink,
to lessen,
to reduce
the space in the chest cavity.

When the chest cavity shrinks on down,
the air that is rich in carbon dioxide
is forced out of your lungs and windpipe,
and then out of your nose or mouth.

And we haven't even gotten
into ventilation
versus respirations.

Because, those aren't the same
even though,
we get it confused.

Ventilations are the movement of a volume of
gas
in and out of the lungs.
Respirations are the
exchange of oxygen and carbon dioxide

across a membrane either in the lungs or at the
cellular level.

Huh.

And all that craziness?

All that movement?

All those amazing inter-workings that
exist to keep us alive that we are oblivious to
when we take our breaths,
that keep us here,
that help us
survive,
thrive,
live,
are all done
involuntarily.

Isn't that simply amazing?

We do something,
that is vital,
to our survival,
and we don't
even actively do it.

So when we wonder what we can do,
when we wonder what we are here for,
when we wonder what is possible...
just think of our body involuntarily working
on our behalf,
just think of our body just trucking
along to make sure
that we are here to do whatever we want.

And....
if our body can
do the miraculous thing of keeping us here,
keeping us alive,
without us even being aware,
or acknowledging it,
then think of the amazing things
we can do
when we put our minds and actions to work.

Breaking

My favorite poet said,
It hurts to become-
and they were right.

But I never knew that fighting to stay here
would unravel me,
causing me to unbecome,
and shatter myself into a million pieces.

Picking Up the Pieces

Shattering ourselves into a million pieces,
isn't the end of the world.

Even though it may be hard work,
even though it bring us back to basics,
even though it may feel like the end.

It just gives us the chance
to create the best mosaic of ourselves that we
can.

Learning Again

My mom asked me to go for a walk.

Before the fog of the darkness, I would spend my days enjoying long hikes for miles but now I struggled to simply find the energy to tie my shoe laces.

We walked together quietly listening to the birds chatter excitedly in the sky, the tires of her walker sliding smoothly on the road and our breath catching for the words we couldn't bring ourselves to say.

I'm sorry I'm like this.

I'm sorry I can't make you better.

She guided her walker to under our best liked tree in the neighborhood.

We loved to watch it's vibrant colors shine through when the colder weather started to blow in.

As she slowly and carefully lowered her body to the chair on her walker I remembered when walking was a goal for her.

A simple back surgery that went terribly wrong.

One surgery that turned into twelve corrective surgeries and 2 years learning to walk again.

Our front door became a revolving door for visiting nurses, occupational and physical therapists.

Our living room was not for relaxing but mile markers to see how far she could walk or if she could reach the remote without falling.

Her little beads of sweat on her forehead always shone so bright when she was in the most pain.

She would grit her teeth while her whole body shook to take a step, her sweat would travel from her forehead, down her nose til it dared to drip off her chin onto the floor.

Sometimes she would wipe it. Other times she would let it fall.

All that strength, all that determination, all the relearning, all the proof in that tiny drop...simply absorbed into the fibers of the carpet never to be seen again.

She didn't need to see it.
She felt it.
She persevered.
She worked through her pain til she could walk again.

We sat in silence for a while.

I watched as she gently pushed herself up when she was ready. She took small steps and led the way.

Maybe just maybe I too could teach myself to walk again.

Cleansing

It was midnight but the time felt right.

I turned on the shower and stood begging the water to wash away this skin I felt trapped in.

The hot water turned cold but I stood still letting the water cleanse me.

It finally woke me up.

I stepped out of the shower and into towels and did my best to wrap myself in love.

Awake I sat in my living room while the night said hello.

Bathed by the moon.

Tickled by the glow of the galaxy.

Fighting the daybreak with all our might.

The calm, tranquility of the night recharged my body like wind uplifting a kite.

Trying Again

Determined soul.
Furiously needing to fly.
Pumping quickly.

Launching forward.
Flying fearlessly through the playground.
Proudly soaring.

Floating downwards.
Sticking the landing, brave arms outstretched.
Greeting the day.

Hopeful Starts

Her eyes are curious but she bites her tongue.

She noticed I was up before her...
and she's trying to figure out if that's good or bad.

She's noticed I've showered,
I'm in clean clothes
and that I've had breakfast.

She spun quickly
but
I still saw her eyes fill with optimistic tears.

And,
it took everything in me
not to break down at the kitchen table.

Moving Forward

I'm accepting that walking aimlessly,
tripping constantly,
finding my path accidentally...

is better than running away gracefully on any
given day.

Progress

You look better

I feel better.

That's what's important.

Going Back

There was a jar on my desk when I returned to work.

I wanted to be professional.
I wanted to be productive.
I wanted to be strong.

In the jar had many folded papers of different sizes and different colors.

The label said if I was having a bad day to reach inside and pick out a paper.

It was a good day.

A weird good day. But I wanted to pick a paper.

I needed to pick a paper.

My fingers fumbled to unfold the little slip and my throat became tight as I read the typed message that said, "Thank you for being here".

I no longer cared to look professional or strong.

I cried, beyond grateful that I chose to stay.

It was a good first day back.

Little by Little

Little by little the days passed.

The numbness wore away.

Nothing changes if nothing changes.

I began to feel again.

Not the best, not the worst.

Not always easy but mostly better.

A work in progress.

Nothing changes if nothing changes.

And I hope to always be a work in progress.

Seeing Clearly

Puddles big and small reflect the periwinkle and golden sky.

The gravel road is designed by carvings from tire tracks and avid walkers.

The soft muddy ground forms shallow basins, offering the melted snow to anyone who would have it.

Bare branches bend and twist in the crisp, whispering winds.

The once proud fourteen foot snow pile has dwindled to a mere one foot, no longer pure white.

Dirtied by the harsh winter and refusing to give up, it still clings to the earth.

A squirrel scurries on the power lines with the goodies he stole from the neighbors' bird feeder puffing his cheeks.

The brown grass is making its debut, certain it will be a lush forest green in no time.

Two small dogs circle the big pine tree on the corner, both trying to claim it as their territory.

One tan, one black. Both emptying any fluid in their bladder to make their mark.

Birds sing cheerfully, and loudly.

The setting sun sets a hazy afterglow on a beautiful day.

Spring is here.
Chance is here.
Change is here.
Life is here.

Finding Light

Darkness is not the enemy.

Refusing to work through it is.

Tomorrow is Today

The woods welcomed me home.

My boots crunch on the earthen floor.
I cannot get enough of the smells and the sounds
of being outside and lost in the joy of exploring.

The sweat drips down my face and I pause to
take a drink.

Looking around I find this a beautiful place to
relax.

Sitting against a strong tree,
I pull out my book, yes that book.
I begin my journey with my favorite characters.

The story I know by heart becomes alive again.

Reminds me to never be a
secondary character in my own story.

Reminds me to always tell my story
even if my voice shakes.|

Smiling, I put down my treasured friend.

When did I start reading again?

I don't remember and I don't need to know.

I'm just glad I made it to my tomorrow.

www.ingramcontent.com/pod-product-compliance
Lightning Source LLC
Chambersburg PA
CBHW051749130826
49812CB00033B/1065
* 9 7 8 9 3 9 5 7 8 4 9 0 0 *